Learn to
DRAW
Dinosaurs

Racehorse for Young Readers books may be purchased in bulk at special discounts for sales promotion, corporate gifts, fund-raising, or educational purposes. Special editions can also be created to specifications. For details, contact the Special Sales Department, Skyhorse Publishing, 307 West 36th Street, 11th Floor, New York, NY 10018 or info@skyhorsepublishing.com.

Racehorse for Young Readers™ is a pending trademark of Skyhorse Publishing, Inc.®, a Delaware corporation.

Visit our website at www.skyhorsepublishing.com.

10 9 8 7 6 5 4 3

Cover and interior artwork: Diego Jourdan Pereira

ISBN: 978-1-63158-240-0

Printed in China

Learn to
DRAW
Dinosaurs

How to Draw Like an Artist in 5 Easy Steps

FOR
YOUNG
READERS

1

2

3

4

5

Practice Page

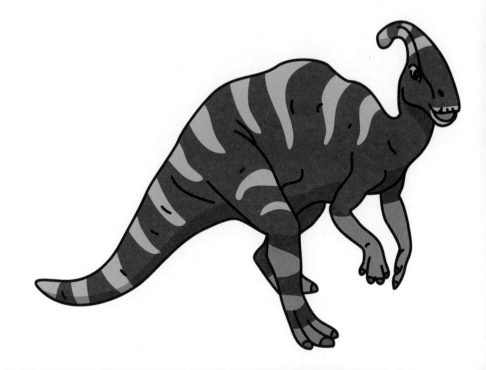

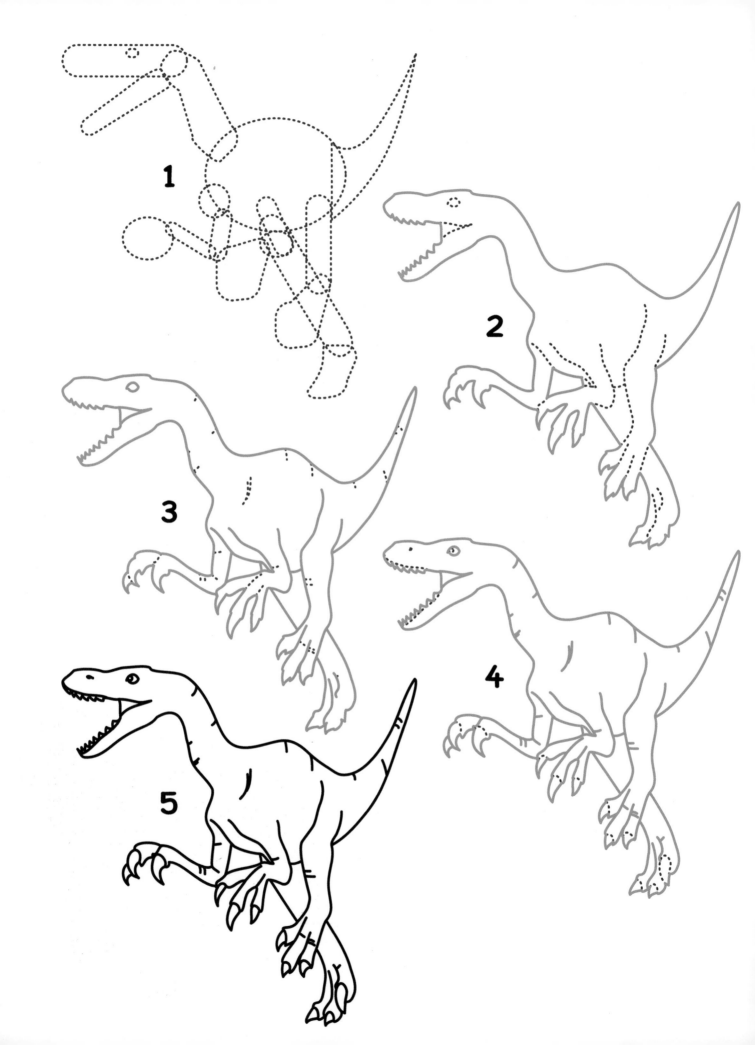

Practice Page

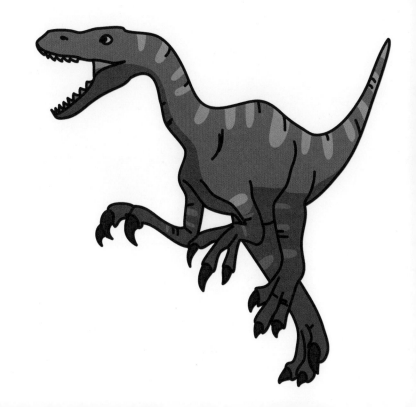

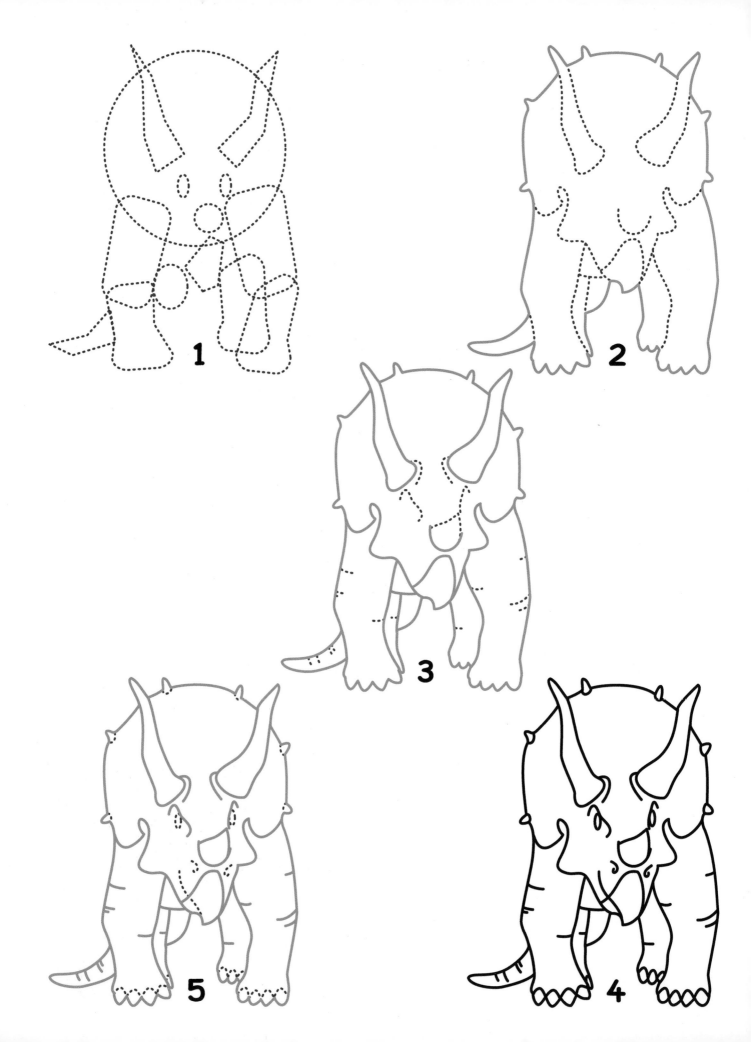

Practice Page

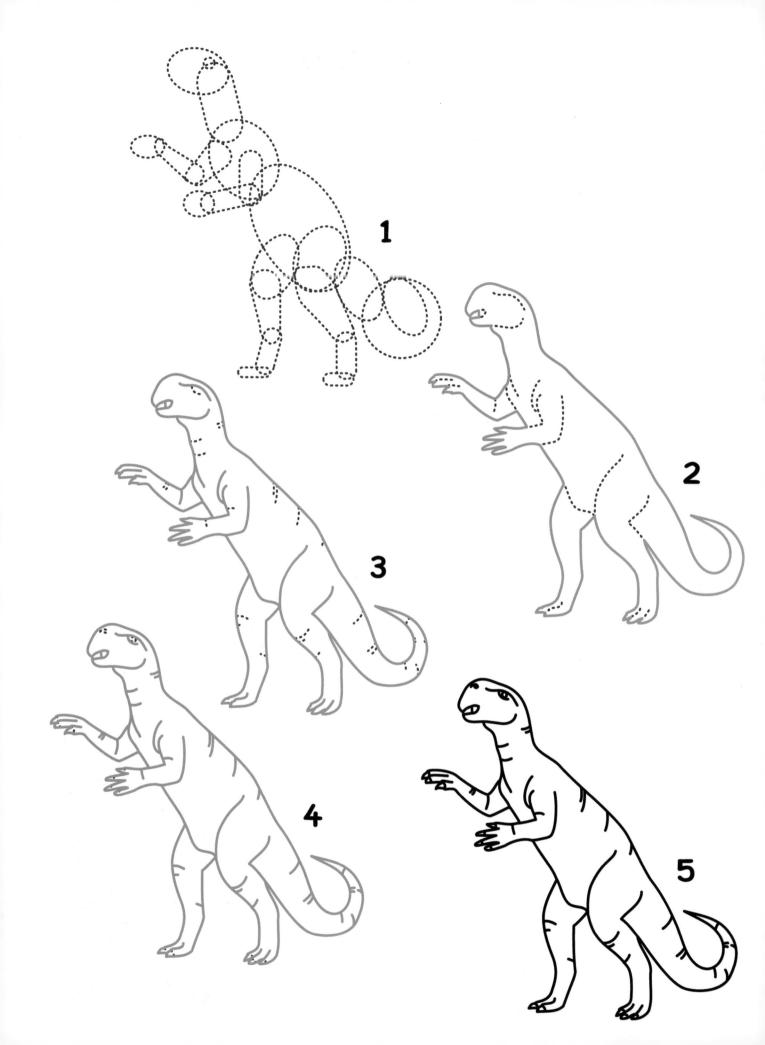

1

2

3

4

5

Practice Page

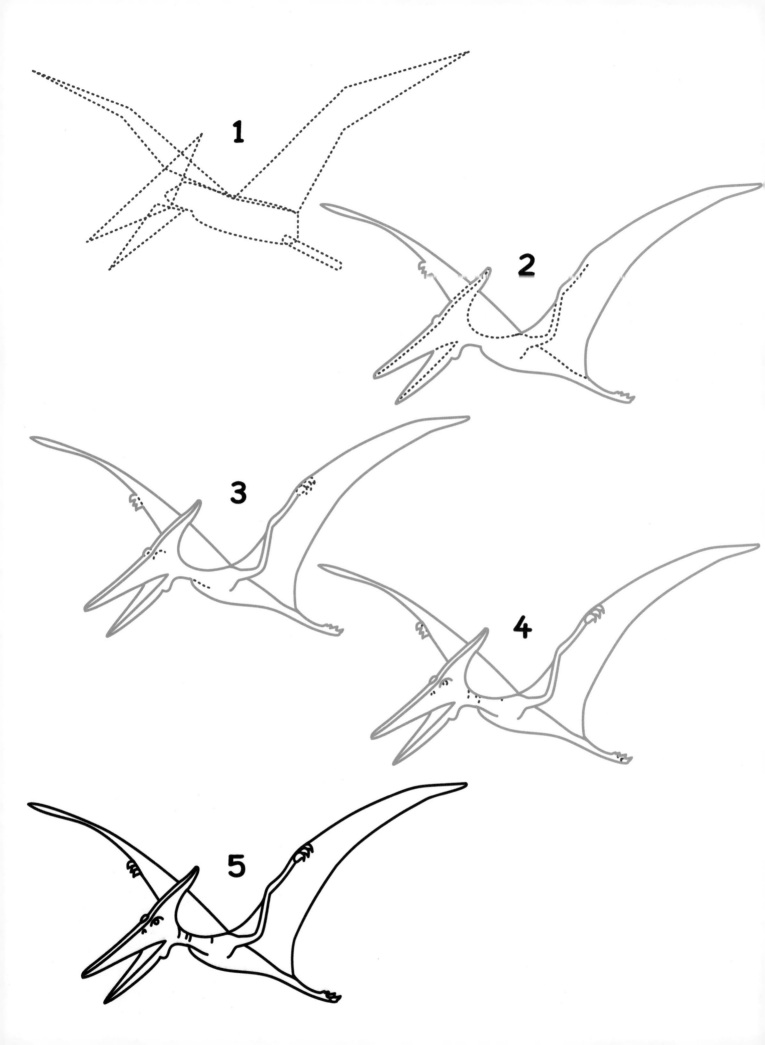

Practice Page

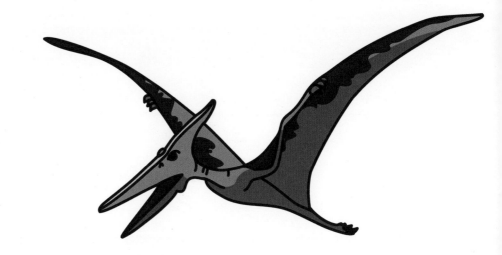

Practice Page

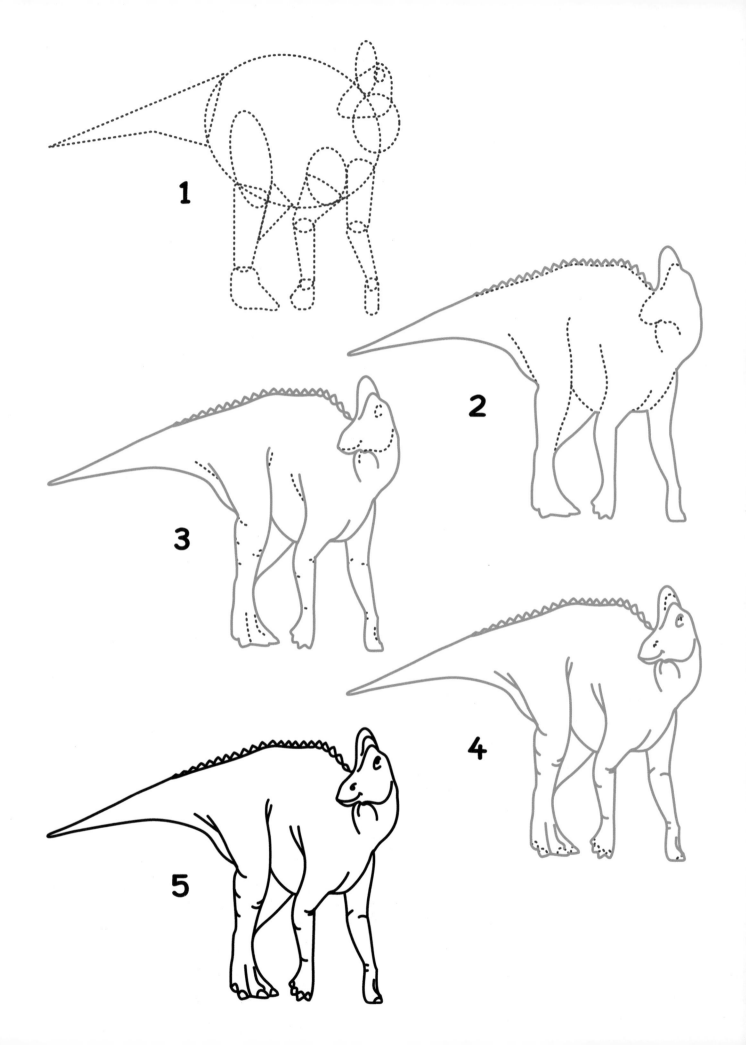

Practice Page

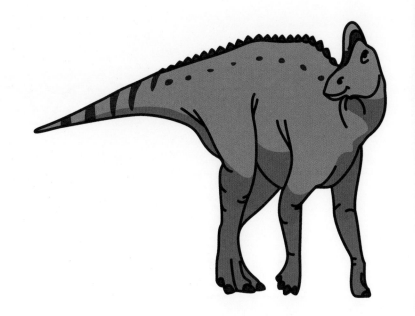

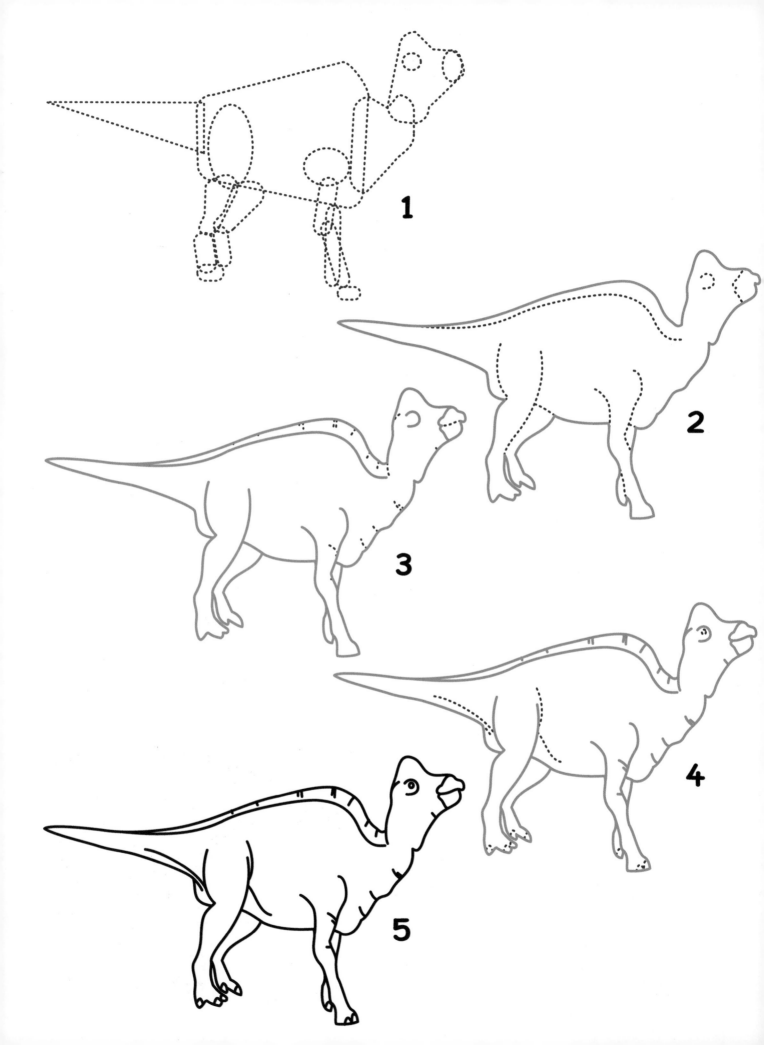

1

2

3

4

5

Practice Page

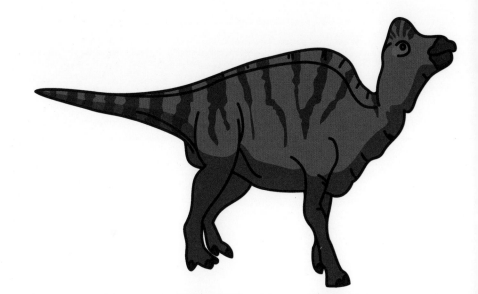

Practice Page

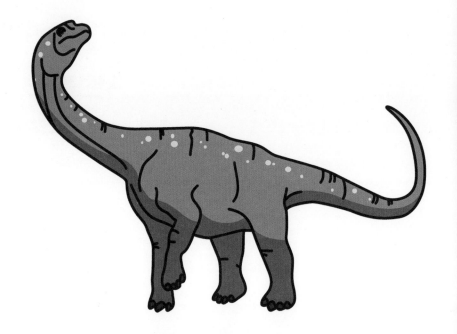

1

2

3

4

5

Practice Page

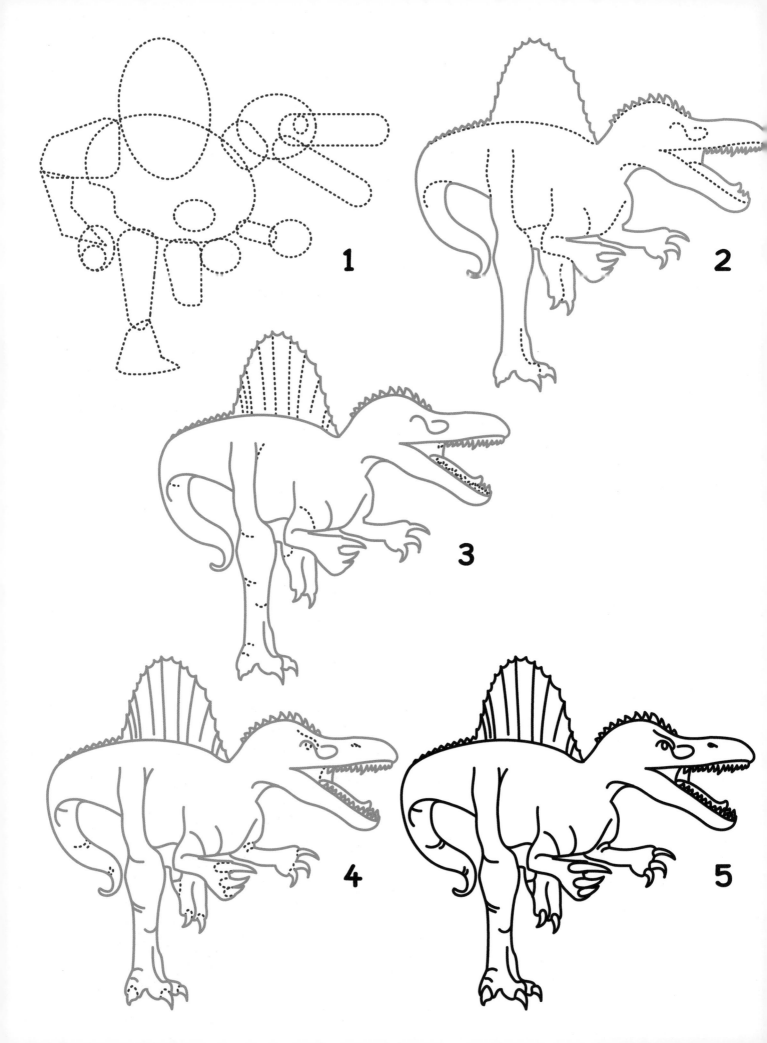

1

2

3

4

5

Practice Page

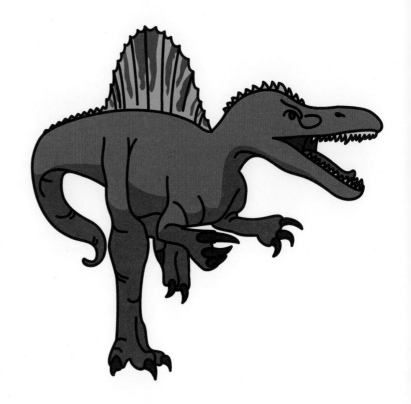

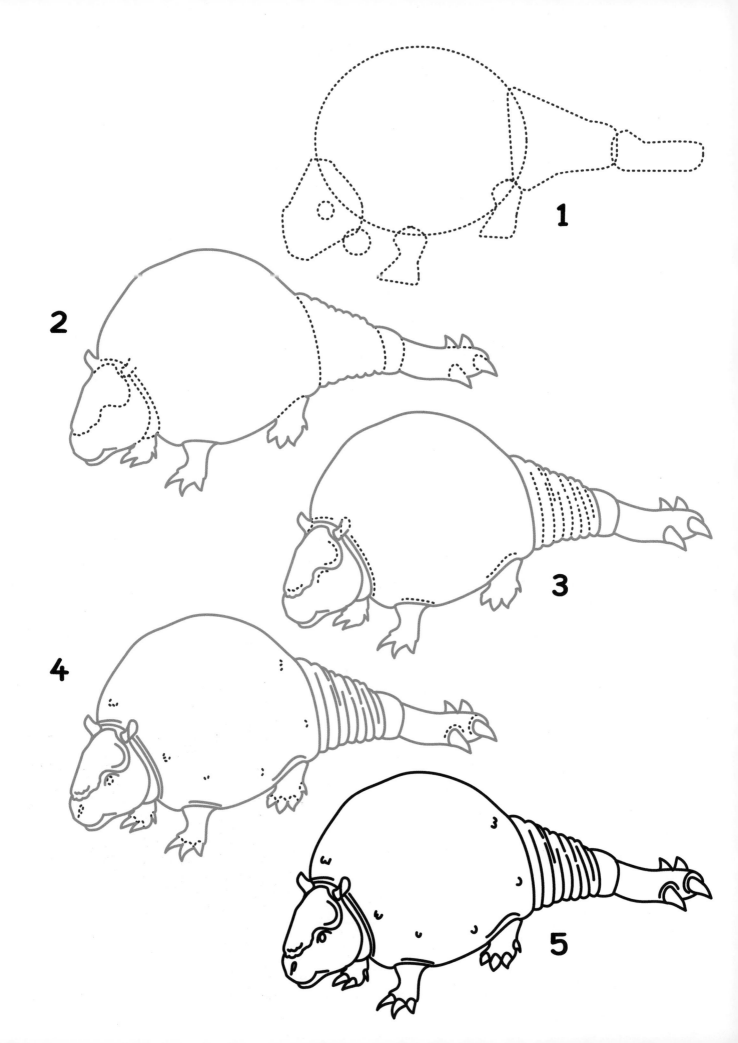

Practice Page

Practice Page

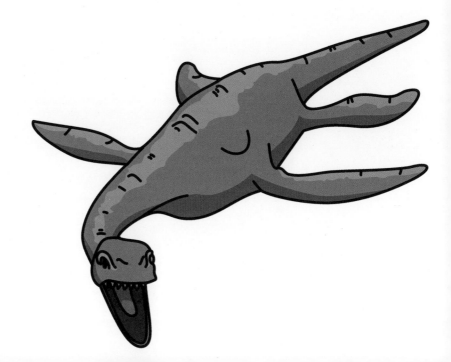

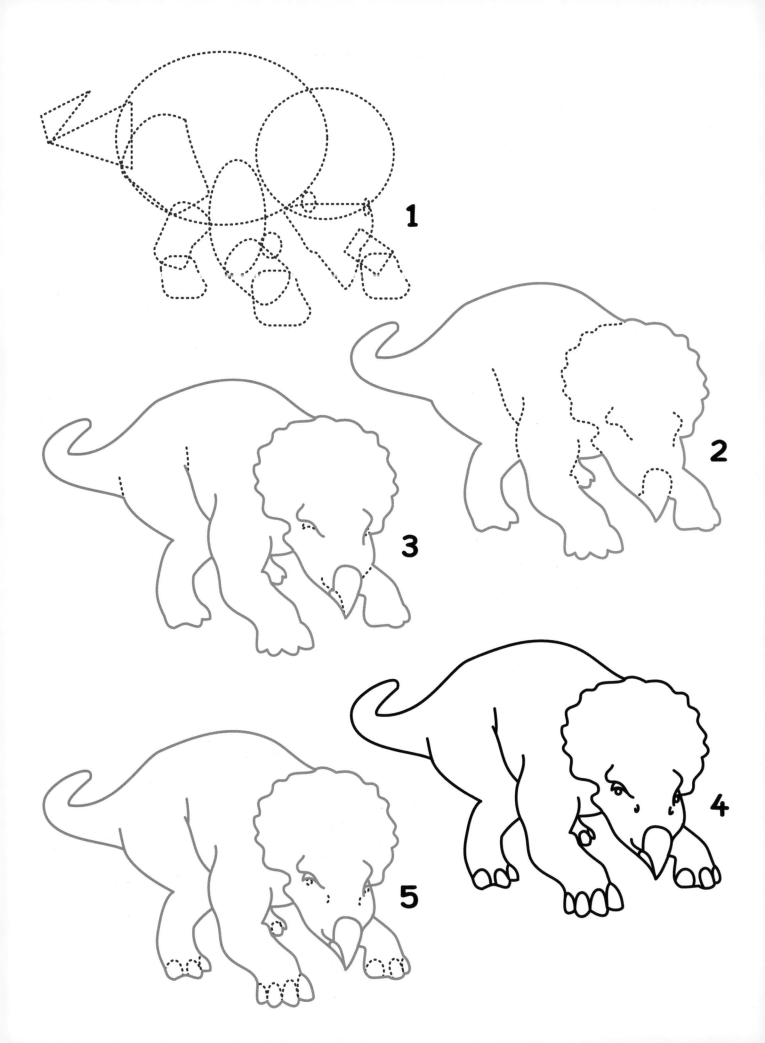

1

2

3

4

5

Practice Page

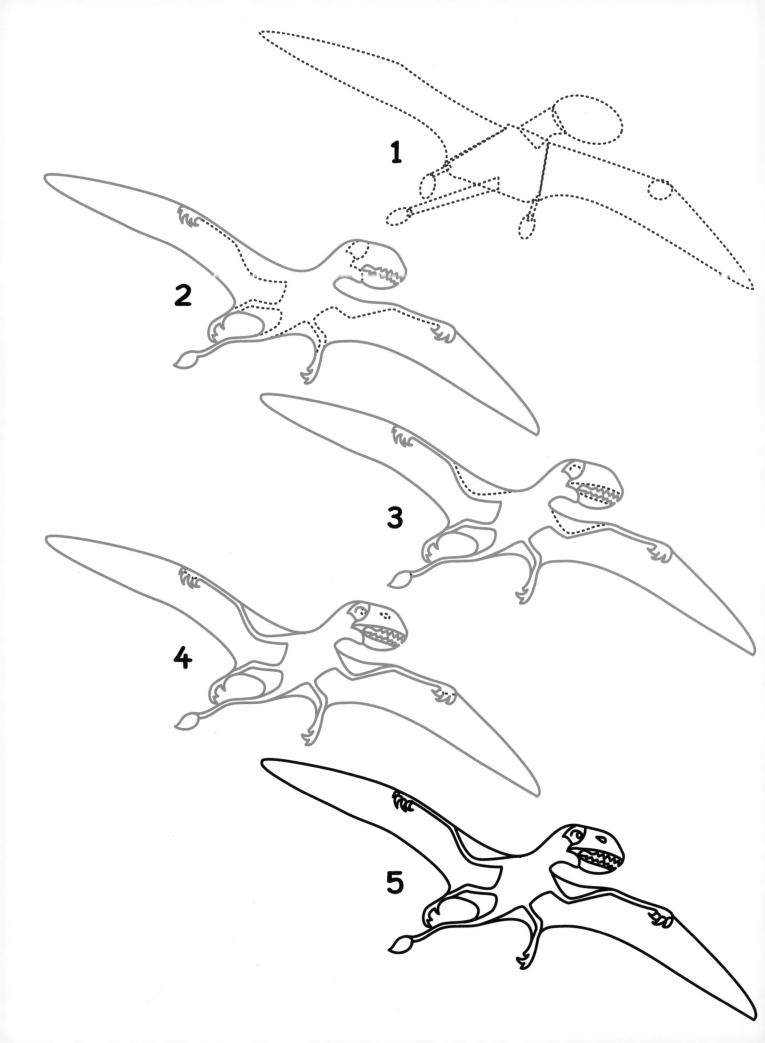

Practice Page

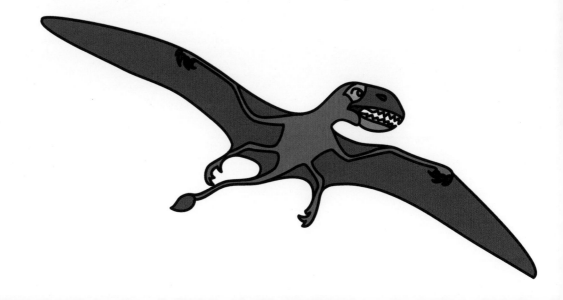

Practice Page

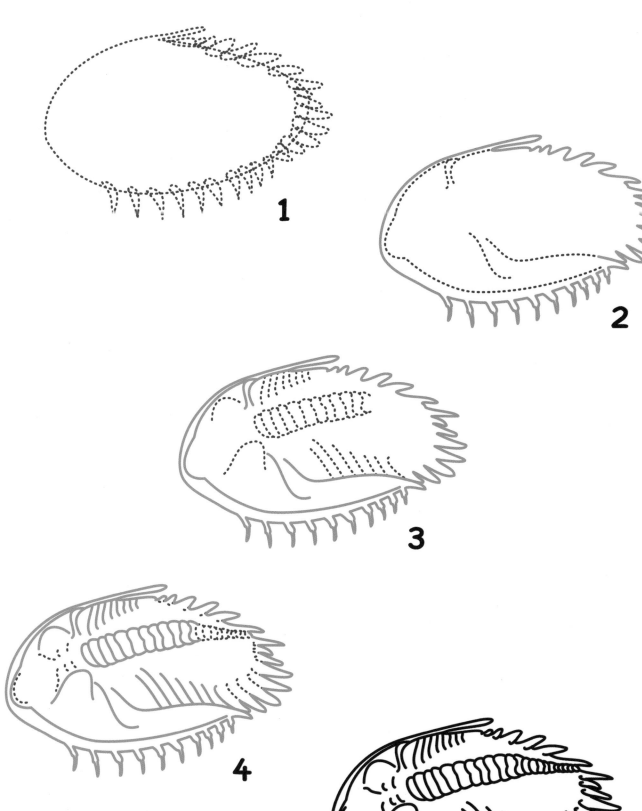

1

2

3

4

5

Practice Page

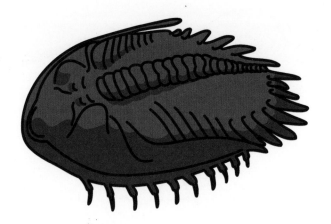

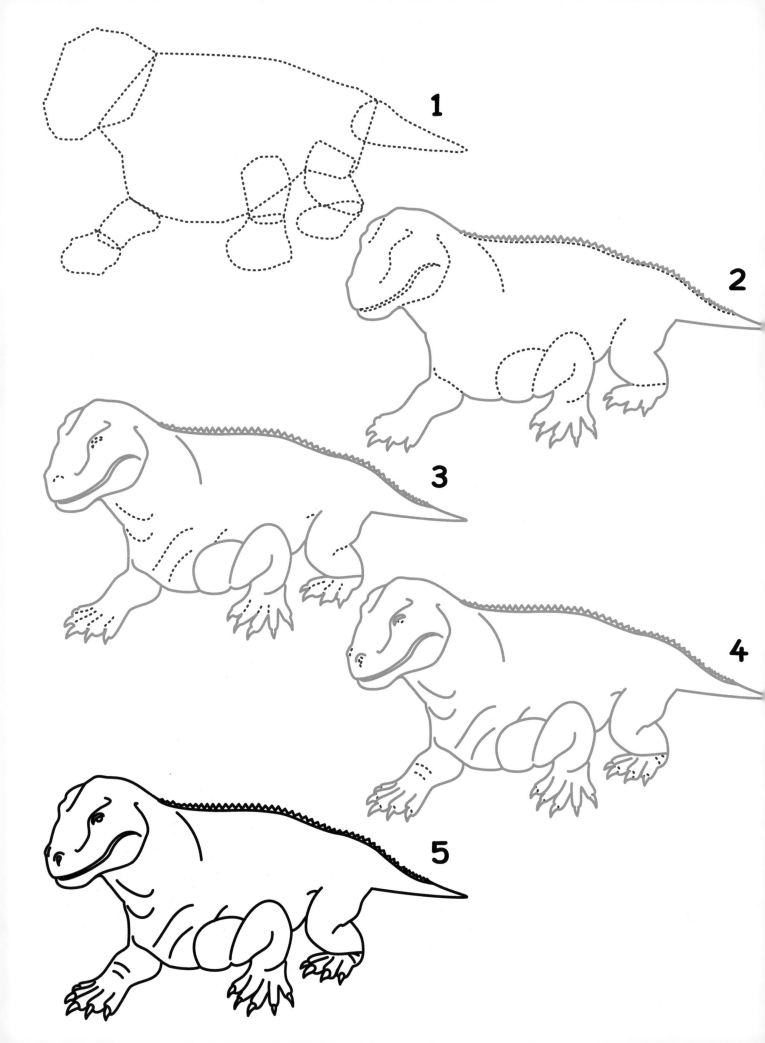

1

2

3

4

5

Practice Page

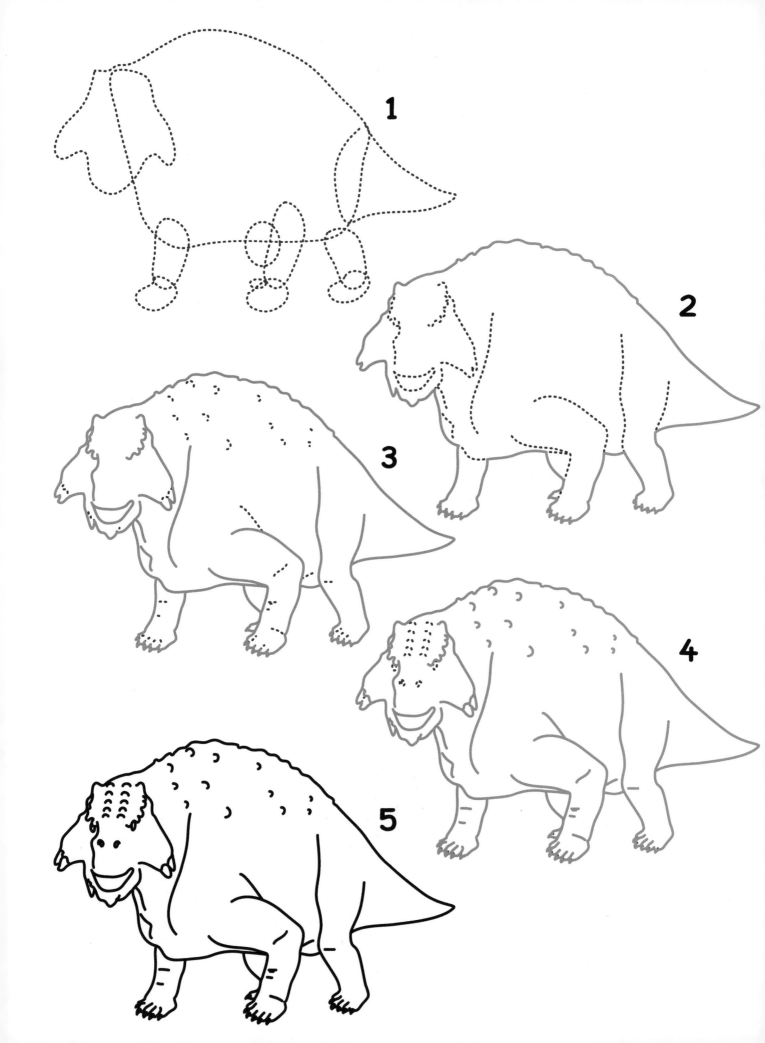

1

2

3

4

5

Practice Page

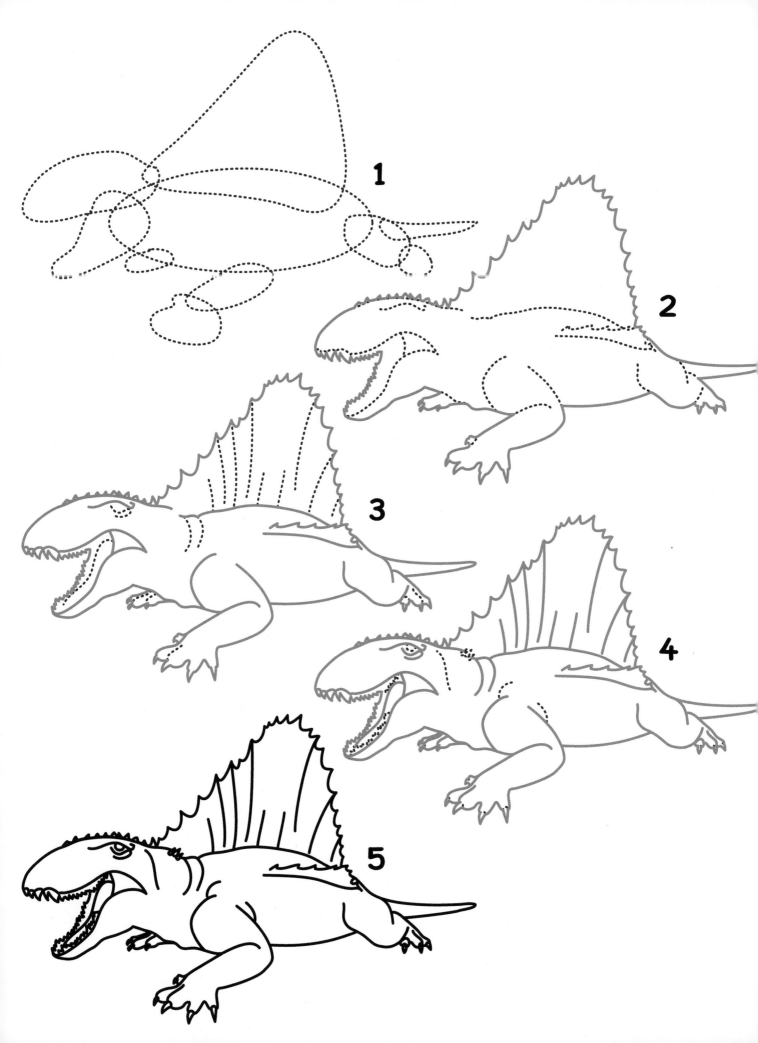

1

2

3

4

5

Practice Page

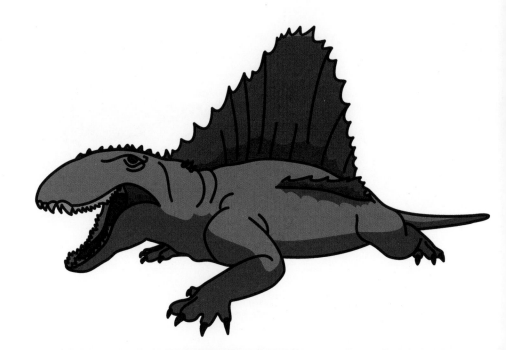

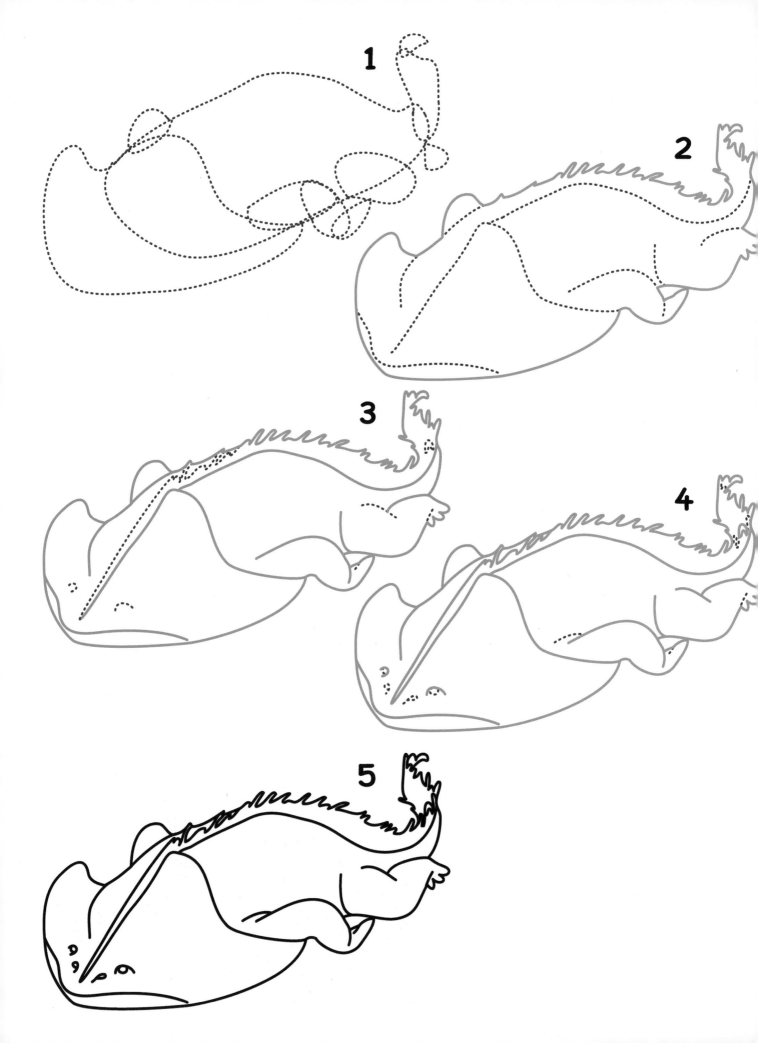

1

2

3

4

5

Practice Page

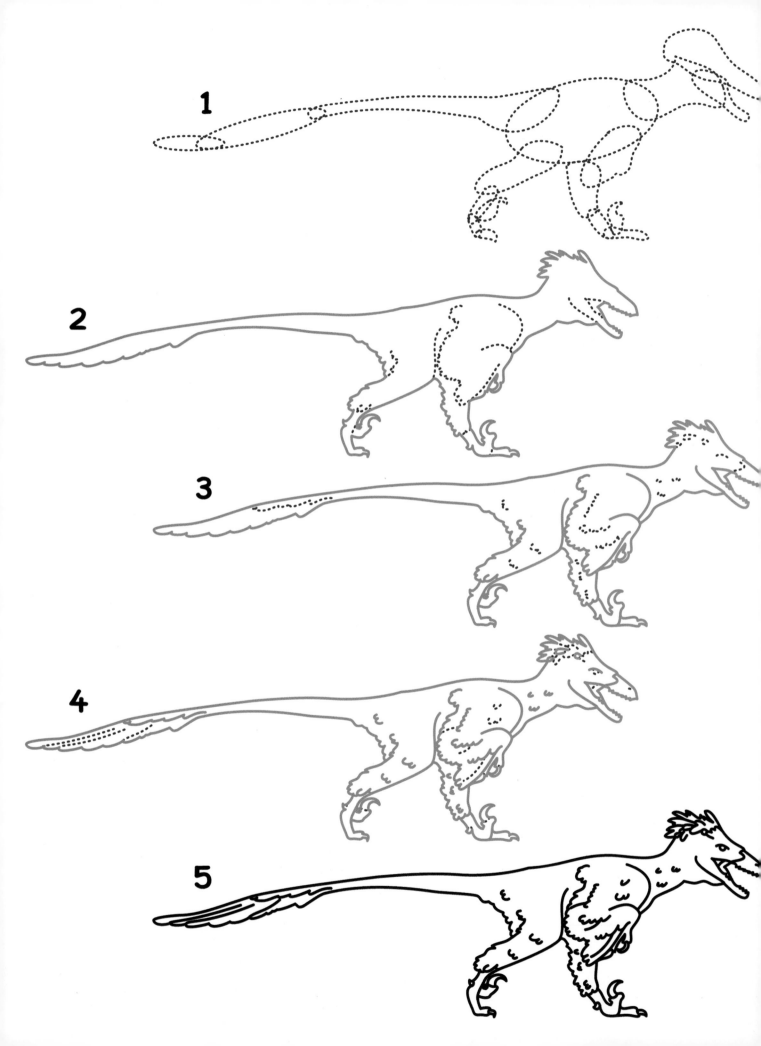

1

2

3

4

5

Practice Page

Practice Page

1

2

3

4

5

Practice Page

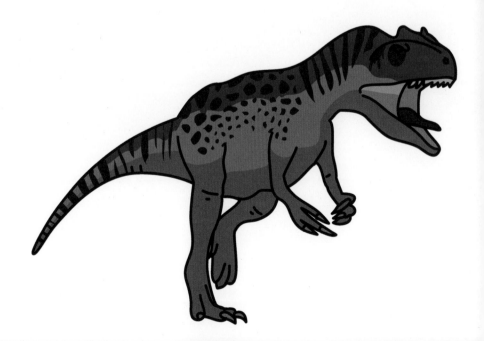

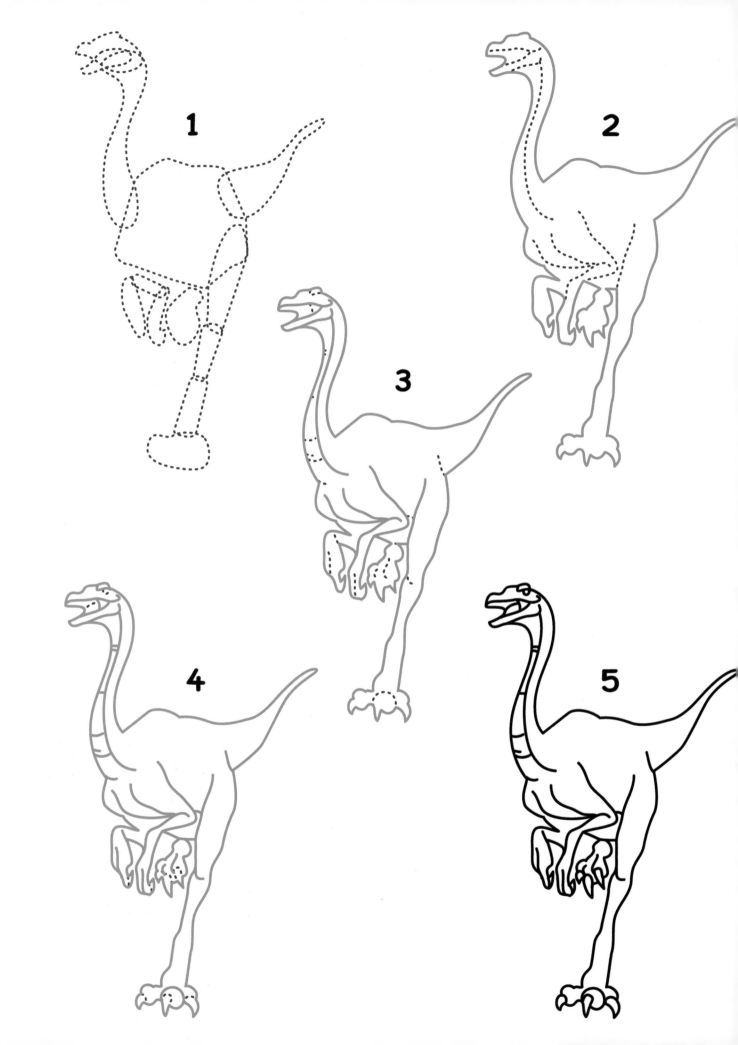

Practice Page

1

2

3

4

5

Practice Page

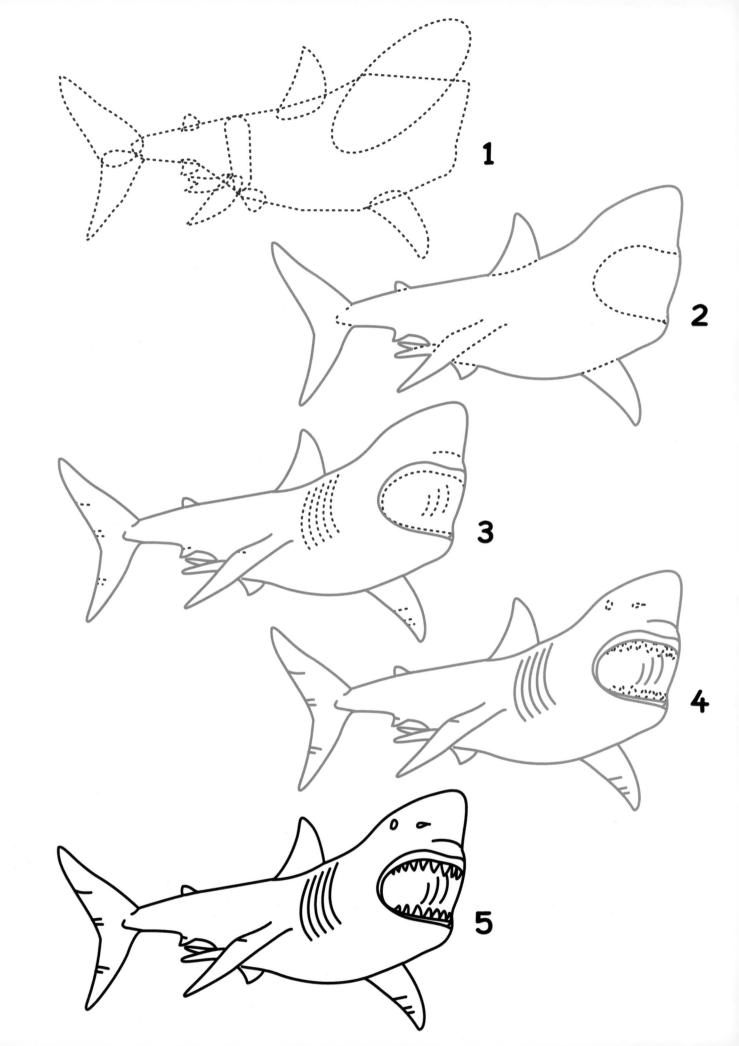

1

2

3

4

5

Practice Page

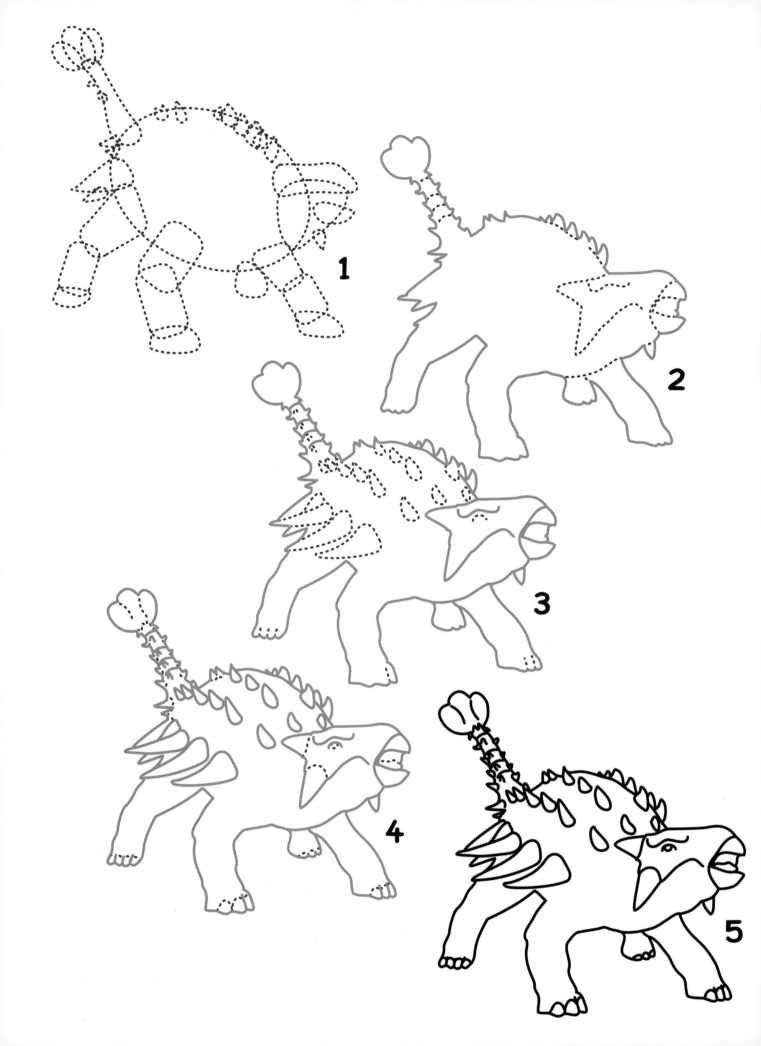

1

2

3

4

5

Practice Page

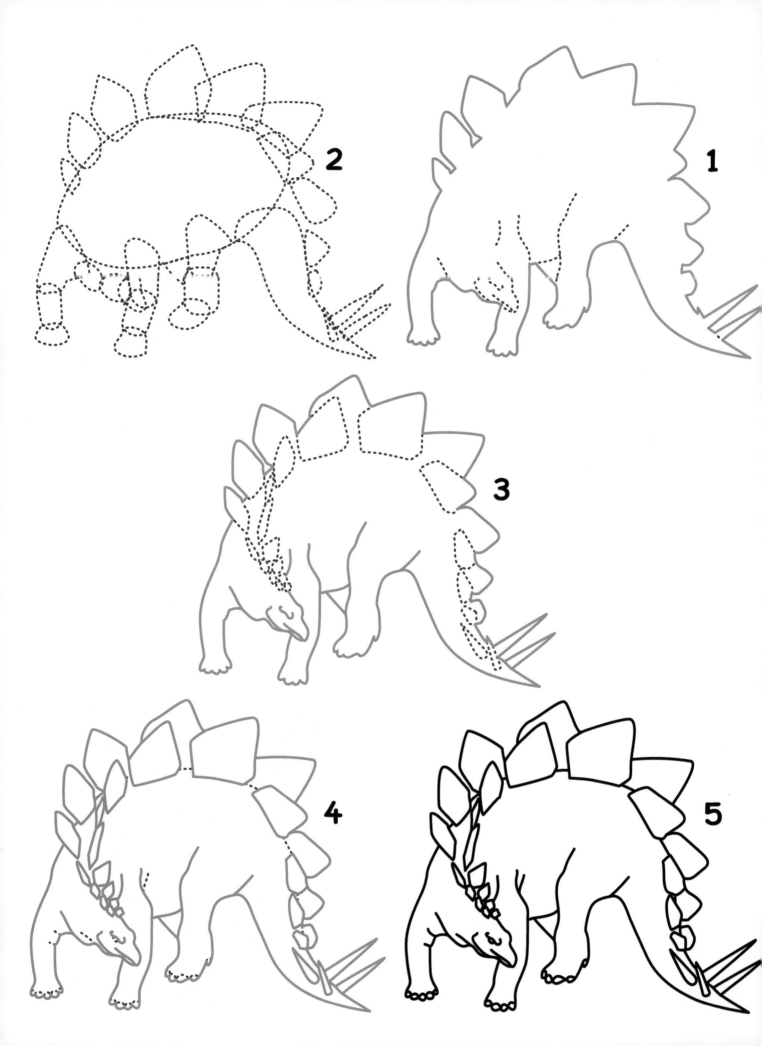

Practice Page

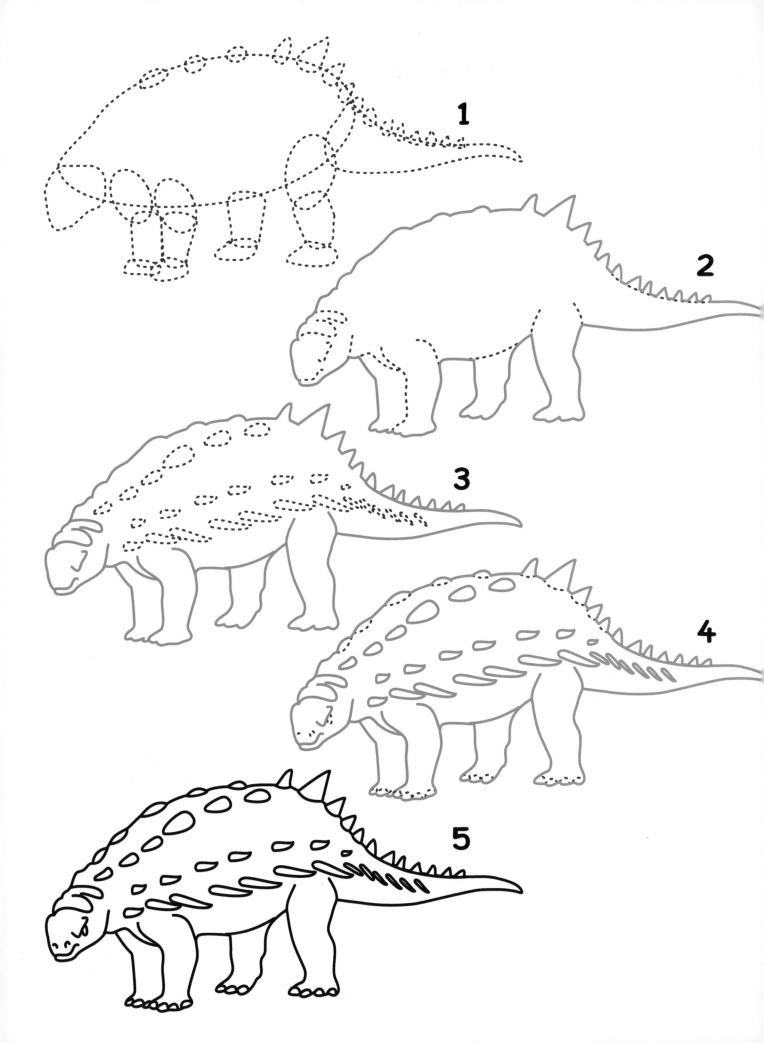

1

2

3

4

5

Practice Page

COLORING PAGES

Practice your new skills here!